Praise for Just Le

"Fierce and compassionate, bold anu resolute, Just Left of the Setting Sun is at once a coming into consciousness as it is a conch-shell blare for action by and for a new generation of Chamorros, the indigenous people of an island and archipelago long colonized by Spain, Japan and the United States of America. As critical towards fellow Chamorros who aid and abet the colonizer as he is of the colonizers themselves, Aguon also importantly situates the need for Native Struggles for Political and Cultural Self-Determination and Sovereignty within Feminist/Womanist critiques and global struggles for economic, social, and environmental justice, thereby providing a glimpse into the possibilities for local struggle informed and articulated to global movements beyond pan-indigenous movements per se, and for keeping global movements and political theory grounded in Indigenous traditions."

Dr. Vicente M. Diaz
Associate Professor of American Culture
University of Michigan, Ann Arbor

"Julian Aguon's work reminds readers that pure and potent colonialism lives on, threatening the island of Guam with ever-more harmful forms of American cultural, political, economic, and ecological disaster. The passionate pages of this volume attempt to shake complacent, colonized readers so that they might realize that the stakes are as high as ever before in the face of American militarization and capitalist globalization."

Dr. Anne Perez-Hattori
Assistant Professor of Pacific History and Humanistic Studies
University of Guam

"...Aguon re-introduces us to the principles of international law as a guiding framework to the resolution of the dilemma brought about by the present non self-governing arrangements which provide the trappings of democratic governance, but in reality are rather democratically deficient by any objective examination. Indeed, an important component of new millennium colonialism is the existence, but not the recognition, of this democratic deficit...

...Just Left of the Setting Sun" should be required reading for the people in the remaining territories, young and old, who need to discover/re-discover the fire within, that they might further move the process forward, if only by a few steps further along the continuum. In a very real sense, as Aguon observes, "inside the heart of the Chamoru is still an ocean of latent potentialities waiting to surge."

Dr. Carlyle Corbin
Advisor on Governance and Political Development
St. Croix, Virgin Islands

The Fire This Time

Essays on Life Under US Occupation

blue ocean press
tokyo

The Fire This Time

Essays on Life Under US Occupation

by

Julian Aguon

blue ocean press
tokyo

Published by:

blue ocean press, an Imprint of Aoishima Research Institute (ARI)
#807-36 Lions Plaza Ebisu
3-25-3 Higashi, Shibuya-ku
Tokyo, Japan 150-0011

mail@aoishima-research.com
URL: http://www.blueoceanpublishing.com
http://www.aoishima-research.com

ISBN: 978-4-902837-11-0

CONTENTS

INTRODUCTION

Tomorrow morning the Department of Defense is scheduled to hand down its master plan, detailing the transfer of thousands of US Marines and their dependents from Okinawa to Guam in a gross - and grossly uncontested - re-occupation of our territory. As test intercontinental ballistic missiles skid across the Micronesian sky and multimillion dollar contracts are pre-awarded to American-based companies for construction work in Guam tied to the transfer, the hope for Chamoru self-determination has never looked so emaciated.

Like the forty petitioners who testified before the United Nations last month for the liberation of Puerto Rico from US occupation, Guam has had no better luck in New York. In a world littered with grave miscarriages of justice, one wonders if the global Left has the left-over energy to add the Territory of Guam to its long carriage of concerns. Another reservoir of moral rage to allow room for ours.

As the indigenous people of the longest colonized island in the entire Pacific, Chamorus are the dispensable backdrop in the global war on terror. Though affectionately known as the place "Where America's day begins," Guam's geopolitical reality as America's westernmost possession is a more telling marker. Our strategic location just north of the equator in the Western Pacific Ocean – the closest piece of American soil to the Orient - is proving vitally important in the face of manic US militarization.

For the Chamorus, this has meant our necessary invisibility. The forgotten lamb tied closest to the war the Pentagon is provoking in Asia, especially now with its hedge strategy aimed at containing China. As regional and national reports suggest, Guam is fast becoming the first-strike target in any altercation between the US and China and/or North Korea.

But the B-2s above is not the loudest noise. The sound of everything we are not saying to each other is even louder. So loud we can barely hear ourselves think. So loud that these essays were written mostly to move into this silence. To get into bed with our timidity and pull back the covers.

Last year I wrote *Just Left of the Setting Sun*, for more than any other practical reason to stop the privatization of Guam's only water provider, the Guam Waterworks Authority. The Guam elite and its puppet media, the Pacific Daily News (PDN), had been waging a yearlong war on public opinion. Selling a lacerated people the lie that privatization (of water and everything else) was in our best interest. Thanks to a dogged few, the concession bill died and the underhanded attempt by the Consolidated Commission on Utilities to allow an outside company to profit off our water systems was defeated.

The usual suspects are back at the betting table. But this time with all the chips.

The Guam Chamber of Commerce, the PDN, and the current Camacho administration, in their joint and unflinching faith in the benefits of US military buildup, are gambling away our genuine security in the name of national security. Through their paper, they have controlled the conversation and outlined - for the rest of us - the landscape of what is and is not the legitimate content of concern. Their bigger trick has been to frame the US military buildup of Guam - its modern colony - in a way that suggests the Chamoru people have real means to right our colonial condition.

55,000 is the latest figure flung at us from on high. This is said to reflect the total number of people relocating to our tiny territory as part of military realignment in the region. This estimate is set to eclipse the Chamoru population one final time. Already, as per the latest CIA calculation, we make up only 37% of the total population of Guam.

These essays are splices of times of intense alert. Moments I was able as writer and as witness to quiet the noise, focus, and pick apart Empire. As best I could.

They are written out of love and in defiance of those forces that seek to destroy a disfigured people. There are those in Guam who mean to crowd out the room for thinking and for possibility. For what it's worth, *The Fire This Time* means to make room.

As information, I hope it lends light on a world kept from the world. On purpose. I hope it lends even more - lends warmth - to my people, who are coming in from the cold and could use it.

Julian Aguon
Guam
July 2006

DEDICATION

For my father Peter Perez Aguon, who history will remember as the one who loved Annabelle, and loved her fiercely.

What we love we can save, including each other, even when we are afraid

The Fire This Time

What Can Be Saved

talk given at the International Gathering of Peace and Justice Activists
Okinawa, Japan
Julian Aguon; June 22, 2006

I have been asked to speak on the current situation of the Chamoru people of Guam, in light of US military realignment schemes now underway in our region. I am here to report: not good.

Last month, US Department of Defense Undersecretary Richard Lawless paid Guam politicians a visit but shared no specifics about how the transfer of more than 8,000 marines and their dependents from Okinawa to Guam will impact our island. To date, defense officials state nothing definite except that Guam is to be a faster response hub to the loose and alleged threats that are China and North Korea. In addition to the marines, we have been informed that the Navy and the Air Force are also making plans to beef up their presence here. The latest is that the Navy may add as many as six additional nuclear submarines on Guam to the three we already house, expand and upgrade naval berthing barges as well as the wharf to accommodate more and bigger vessels. It plans to add a sixth aircraft carrier and to home port sixty percent of its Pacific Fleet in the region.

The Air Force is working to establish a Global Strike Force on Guam, which will include Global Hawk unmanned reconnaissance aircraft, deployed bombers, tankers, F/A-22 fighter jets and other aircraft. Deputy Commander of the US Pacific Command Daniel Leaf informed us of programs in work to establish a strike and intelligence surveillance reconnaissance hub at Andersen Air Force Base on the northern end of our island. Though this buildup is massive, it is only a complement to the already impressive Air Force and Navy show of force on 1/3 of the island, which now threatens to make Guam a first-strike target in any altercation with China and/or North Korea.

The recent announcement that the US and Japan finalized negotiations on the relocation of the marines that you here in Okinawa are kicking out, was greeted by the Guam elite with fanfare. They want them. Actually, they have been flagging them down. Our governor and his republican-led administration, the local Chamber of Commerce (consisting primarily of US statesiders), and the press have been up to their elbows in excitement ever since the announcement was made. The elite have launched a propaganda campaign to trick us into believing that the corporatization and militarization of Guam is in our community's best interest. Back home, editorials telling half-truths and little-to-none truths sound like trumpets in the territory. Articles that passionately support the privatization of virtually every public agency and that lay bare a blind faith in the benefits of military buildup rain down on the readership, as our little piece of Gannet, the Pacific Daily News, is up to its old habit: down on its knees in its endless genuflection toward corporate America.

Its reporters still pretend to report the news and the line, with little variation, remains: privatize everything – our one and only water provider, only power provider, only local telephone provider, and only port - on an island that imports 85-90% of its food and where private monopolies of public goods would truly make it captive to the forces of the market. To bring you up to speed, telecommunications were sold in full, our power distributor in part, and our water agency is still under attack. After an incompetent piece of legislation that would have had an American-based company profit off our water systems was defeated last year, the elite pushed an alternative mode of privatization. Recently, a private management contract was authorized to outsource the management of the agency's wastewater division. Meanwhile, the Port Authority of Guam has been taken to court by a private, foreign company for allegedly acting in bad faith with regard to its Request for Proposal. All this painted as part and parcel of readying Guam for an increased US military presence. A classic story of corporate globalization: the integrity of an ancient civilization on sale to the lowest bidder.

But the story of the 212 square mile island affectionately called the 'tip of the spear' in the US line of defense begs a bit more history.

Situated just north of the equator in the Western Pacific Ocean, Guam is the southernmost island of the Mariana Island Chain, in Micronesia. The native people of Guam call ourselves and our language Chamoru. We are descendents of the first group of Austronesians to move eastward into Oceania, populating our island archipelago long before others would reach island groups east of Micronesia. We were master navigators, matrilineal and, in 1521, Magellan's first Pacific contact. The plot, tragically, does not change much from here. Colonized by Spain for more than three hundred years, awarded to the US after Spain's defeat in 1898 as one of its Treaty of Paris prizes (its others being Puerto Rico, Cuba, and the Philippine Islands), taken by Japan in the second world war only to be re-taken by the US at its close, Guam has since been subject to administration by the Office of Insular Affairs in the US Department of Interior.

As one of the few remaining non-self-governing territories (colonies) of the world, Guam today waits on a miracle - on US compliance with international law. Current US military operations in our region are a continuation of a long disregard for international law, which holds the US, as our Administering Power, legally responsible to protect the Chamoru people until the right to self-determination is exercised. As a signatory of the United Nations Charter, the US accepted as "a sacred trust" the obligation to see that the native inhabitants of Guam attain a full measure of self-government. More than forty years ago, UN Resolution

1514 was passed, declaring that 'all peoples have the right to self-determination; by virtue of that right they freely determine their political status and freely pursue their economic, social and cultural development.' It declared further that "immediate steps shall be taken, in Trust and Non-Self-Governing Territories or all other territories which have not yet attained independence, to transfer all powers to the peoples of those territories, without any conditions or reservations, in accordance with their freely expressed will and desire."

The last forty six years have slowly stripped the words of their weight.

Back home, war games are afoot. As I speak, three US aircraft carriers - the USS Abraham Lincoln, the USS Kitty Hawk, and the USS Ronald Reagan – are playing what have been casually called war games. To date, no information has been released to the government of Guam on the contents of these games. As these ships engage in military exercise Valiant Shield, doing only God knows what, local leaders are simply waiting on word as to whether or not one of the three flattops will make a port call. Pump dollars into the local economy. The only thing we know about the exercise is that it is not limited to these vessels; defense officials report that 22,000 U.S. military personnel, 30 ships and 280 aircraft will partake in the exercise.

In all this, our leaders are nowhere to be found, except maybe in the private homes of the Guam elite, making toasts to the triumph of the free market. Shamelessly usurping the patriotism of a war-worn people. Or maybe they are busy missing meetings. Our governor is notorious for this. Last month, after snubbing a politician from Okinawa who visited Guam to discuss the transfer of the marines, Governor Camacho canceled two meetings with the Japanese government. Mikio Shimoji, member of both Japan Diet's Committee on Foreign Affairs and Committee on Security, tried in vain to meet with him. When pressed for an answer, he said that he was taking a "conservative approach." He publicly admitted that he was waiting on a response from US federal officials, who he asked to establish a protocol for visits by foreign officials, so that he doesn't "step over any lines."

Earlier in his term, our governor missed the UN regional seminar on decolonization. In a letter to the UN Special Committee on Decolonization Chairman Julian Hunte, he implied that Guam was working with the US on its self-determination at the domestic level and that there was no pressing need to work with the international community on this matter.

He is not the only one who dodged meetings with Japan last month. He and our non-voting representative to Congress, Madeleine Bordallo, agreed not to meet with any foreign officials until after they had met with Undersecretary of Defense Lawless. Bordallo told reporters that the rationale behind the decision not to entertain foreign guests was that "this is the time when we're working on details." She must know something no one else does. The same day, US defense officials made it clear that no details could be shared with the people of Guam because no details were yet known.

So, what do we know?

That the Navy now playing war games off our waters is the same one that contaminated our waters, our lands and our livers with an older version of the same game.

Almost immediately after the last world war, the US conducted a series of nuclear experiments in Micronesia. A report released by the committee commissioned by the 26th Guam Legislature to investigate how Guam was affected by the US bombing of the Marshall Islands between 1946 and 1958, detailed strong evidence of potential radioactive contaminations of our home. Guam, 1200 miles west of the Marshalls, received nuclear fallout from more than ten of the sixty-six bombs dropped on Enewetak alone. US military vessels flown above the plumes of Enewetak to measure radioactivity were flown to Guam and flushed out. To date, the toxics at Apra Habor and Cocos Lagoon on Guam have yet to be cleaned. The Guam Environmental Protection Agency recently issued a public warning to refrain from eating fish in that area due to dangerous levels of cancer-causing dioxins in the water. Just last year, east of us, four Marshallese babies born without eyeballs reminded the world of these transgressions.

Reports of related contamination are coming in from all over. Recently in Harris County, Texas, a retired US-Navy Lieutenant - riddled with a fifty-year-old guilt – declared before a Notary Public that Guam received radioactive fallout from the first hydrogen bomb test done in the Marshall Islands. Bert Schreiber, the Atomic, Biological, and Chemical Warfare Defense Officer stationed in Guam at the time of the first series of bombings, gave written testimony that on the morning of November 3, 1952, after discovering radioactive material from an H-bomb dropped on Enewetak atoll two days prior, his superior ordered him to keep his mouth shut. The deadly dust fell on a people who could have taken at least some precautionary measures. Only last month, another defense official informed us of how the US kept about 5,000 drums of Agent Purple in Guam in an undisclosed area in 1952 in anticipation of use on the Korean peninsula. According to a researcher who participated in a military experiment in Guam in the sixties, the amount of dioxin at Andersen Air Force Base alone indicates a disturbing degree of US military irresponsibility (or is it indifference?) Further investigation awaits commission.

But the bands play on and we are expected to believe that the danger is China, North Korea. Iran too. I almost forgot: we should forget the fact that every single reason the US used to justify it's going to war with Iraq has turned out a lie. While we're at it, we might as well hate Cuba and downplay the acts of political bravery rippling across leftist Latin America, lest we see them for what they are: shining acts of self-determination hurled at the myth of free market inevitability. But I am getting a little ahead of myself. Contemporary politics back home doesn't have that wide a reach. In the Guam of today, political science is more a story of mirrors and a people's facelessness in them.

But what we really came to say is simple. The Chamoru Nation is here because we intend to survive. We are also here to renew our pact with you to actively encourage the withdrawal of the exaggerated US military presence from all – not some – of our communities. To declare to the world what we know: that the aggressive militarization of our region is laying humanity a premature grave. And we find that unacceptable.

Solidarity is not our best bet. It is our only one. As an international gathering of peace and justice activists, we are building momentum for the global demilitarization movement. In the process, I hope we are building a better bridge across the world we are working toward and the weed of cynicism gaining too much ground in human hearts.

I pray for the builders. That we keep our courage close. This world we are building from the bones of ideas that have failed humanity has set us out on an unkind wind. Our sisters and brothers here from the Philippines know this better than most. All across that country, democracy is under attack, civil liberties are being curtailed, death squads kill freely and the administration of President Arroyo practically sanctions them. Since 2001, more than six hundred people – human rights workers, journalists, priests, lawyers, teachers, labor leaders, students – have been murdered. More than a hundred and fifty disappeared. Their crime? Thinking. And having the courage to align a life with their hunger for justice. Doing its part in the vague 'global war on terror', the Arroyo administration has *Oplan Bantay Laya*, a program aimed at neutralizing (destroying) what is really the people's progressive movement. For its counterinsurgency efforts, the US gave that government $30 million dollars in one year alone.

You folks in Okinawa have shouldered your share of suffering. As Washington's top ally (alley) cat in East Asia, Japan continues to negotiate away your freedom from harm, bodily and otherwise. Japan leadership has yet to listen to the logic living in your rage. Playing host to 75% of the total US troops stationed in Japan has pushed your patience – and your nonviolence – to its limits.

As you scream about the noise and the rape and the alcoholism and the violence of the US military presence in your cramped home, US defense officials tell senators back home that the marines being moved to Guam are family-oriented. That the feds will work with us to ensure the transfer is a "win-win" situation. The Boston Herald reports that even after the 8,000 troops are transferred, about 15,500 will remain here.

But in the end this is not our end. The proponents of justice will outlast the proponents of privatization, militarization, and death. Because all empires fall. Because enough of us realize or will realize that a choice must be made. Either we pursue justice or we perish. And because we know the truth:

What we love we can save, including each other, even when we are afraid.

The Last Corner on Earth

The deal recently struck between the governments of the United States and Japan allowing for the transfer of 8,000 marines and their dependents should scare us but not into silence.

The people of Guam are right to be outraged at how people in power, our own included, are having a conversation about us but not with us. This move will affect the entire landscape of our future and our children's future yet we are expected to keep quiet about it. When we will realize that keeping quiet is killing us? Why are our leaders so quick to welcome the same troops being kicked out of Okinawa? Why would we want the same marines who terrorized those citizens with rape, alcoholism, noise pollution and violence?

Local leaders unable or unwilling to see that this move will cause our island great social, cultural, and ecological harm - raising societal violence to likely devastating heights - keep saying this transfer is good for Guam. The answer to our economic prayer. It appears again that money is the only thing making the grade, filling the ranks of things worth worrying about.

What is it going to take for us to find our feet and stand against this gross re-occupation of our island? Is it going to take the raping of our women, which is not only a possibility but a near guarantee? Is it not foolish to think that the same troubles harassing the people of Okinawa will not cause us similar distress?

Beyond the inherent violence of militarism is a fact as clear as day. China's one brow is raised at us already. Reports coming in from around the region suggest that China competently discerns what the US military buildup of Guam and the Northern Mariana Islands means. A finger of portent pointed at China to provoke her, not contain nor deter her. It seems we are the only ones who do not understand that Guam is little more than the sacrificial lamb in US military realignment schemes. Intelligence too clearly indicates it. Whether we read the Washington Times or the Okinawa Times, USA Today or the Yomiuri Shimbun, we get it. The recent publication of the National Defense

Research Institute prepared for the Office of the Secretary of Defense also lends a light. Across the mediums, the fact floating always to the top is this: our strategic location is only strategic to the US, which needs us more than its defense department cares for us to know.

What about the war this buildup will wage on our environment? The same government our leaders are welcoming is the same one that has yet to clean its contamination of our land and water during and after the last world war. The same one set to move more weapons of mass destruction and toxins to these parts. The same one that owes millions in war reparations due to us since our alleged liberation of 1945, when the legal responsibility to pay reparations was transferred to the US under the provisions of the treaty it signed with Japan at the close of World War II. The same one still that used our fellow Micronesians as human guinea pigs in its horrific nuclear experiments from which everyone in the region still suffers- in the form of disproportionate rates of radioaction-related cancers.

It is no coincidence that Guam is a Superfund darling. In the central and south, the Navy has not cleaned up either Cocos lagoon or Apra Harbor, which we know is among the worst contaminated sites in all of Guam. In the north, Andersen Air Force Base discharges dioxins almost casually and the major portion of US land holdings sits atop or adjacent to the northern aquifer, our primary source of potable water. How many northern wells have been shut down because of chemical contamination? North of Guam, in Saipan, ceramic capacitors leaking polychlorinated biphenyls (PCBs) were discovered not too long ago in Tanapag village. According to regional reports, the capacitors, transferred by the US defense department from the Marshall Islands to Saipan in 1967, came from one of its missile installations on Kwajalein atoll. Twenty years passed before the US informed the local government of the danger. How many more cancer-causing agents are now leaking, floating, spilling all over the terrain of unasked questions caught at the tip of our tongue?

Are we not tired of burying our dead?

We cannot be naïve enough to believe our high cancer rates are not connected to US military contaminations of our region. Nor can we believe that the same government will discontinue its use of our archipelago as the site of future experiments. In the end, a search for short-term economic stimulus is welcoming added crimes against humanity.

If we're following the cover story closely, more split ends.

The figures get fatter. Though originally estimated at 7,000 marines, a thousand more were thrown in since last year. Joining the now 8,000 marines will be their 9,000 dependents. Now, both the Navy and the Air Force want in and last week it was announced that 5,000 of them and their dependents will add to the 17,000 pot. The latest figure flung down from the feds is 35,000, said to represent the total number of US military personnel, support staff, and dependents destined for Guam by 2014. This announcement came with another. Now, because Guam does not have big enough a workforce to take advantage of the construction projects the buildup will bring, an outside labor force estimated upwards of 20,000 will join the 35,000. That's 55,000.

So, more people are set to flood the territory as part of this buildup than there are total Chamorus living in Guam. Unless Chamorus living in the continental US come home, and soon, there will be no time to ready a local labor force to take advantage of these developments. We are already a minority. What more, 2014? When this thing is done, and if its ultimate end is accomplished, Guam will not be Guam because she will be without her people. And if we actively participate in this importing of the forces of our death, the colonization will have killed us. Seeped too deep. Ate our insides and emptied us out.

Or has this ship already made it to shore?

Chamorus today make up only 37% of the 171,019 total people living in Guam. Though minorities in our home, we - somehow - manage to be overrepresented in the various branches of the US military, in the Guam homeless count, in the local prison, in cases of domestic violence, HIV/AIDS, and public assistance. The latest Salvation Army study (Jan. 05) found almost a thousand homeless folks living in the cracks of Guam society. In the span of thirty two miles, more than three hundred families flounder. At just over 48%, Chamorus are the lone exaggerated ethnic group in last year's homeless count. Over double the percentage of the closest follower.

Down at the jailhouse, the story gets worse. We make up more than 90% of all incarcerations.

With the HIV/AIDS epidemic en route to this region via Indochina, the global health community worries that we, and the rest of Micronesia, will not be able to stand up under the weight of the killer when it comes. A legitimate worry. We lead this region in the health care industry and we all know just how close our one hospital keeps coming to closure. In this arena, Chamorus are most of the 185 people who have tested positive for the virus since 1985. Most of the people living with the virus today. We figure survival sex is part of the stuff of life in the cracks.

These are the kinds of signs on the walls around us, closing in.

Today this transfer is being sold to us as good, even necessary. The rescue we've been waiting for. Military buildup is being framed in a way that suggests we have real choices here. But people without real means to right their colonial condition know that this tale is a tall one.

The deal recently struck between the governments of the United States and Japan allowing for the transfer of now 55,000 people to Guam should scare us into a world of questions, a world afire with inquiry.

The last corner on earth it should scare us into is silence.

She has been no friend to us.

A Lonely Gantry Crane

Last week I attended a thesis defense of a group of graduate students in the business school on the privatization of the Port Authority of Guam (PAG). To cut to the quick, they concluded that it makes no sense to privatize our one and only commercial port. From a purely financial stance, it is irrational to privatize the only real revenue-making public entity. In fact, PAG has been increasing its net assets for the last two fiscal years.

In 2004, it increased its net assets by $1.9 million dollars. PAG closed last fiscal year with net assets of 46.8 million, a further increase of $489,000 from the previous year. If PAG was left alone and allowed to operate as the autonomous public corporation it was intended to be since Public Law 13-87 was passed in 1975, it would have even more money. But this is not the case. The group reported that between 1994 and 1998 GovGuam transferred about $10 million dollars from PAG to the General Fund and continues to eye PAG money whenever GovGuam is strapped for cash.

Despite the hype, the problems at PAG boil down to one lonely gantry crane more than anything else. The cost to replace the broken crane is about $7 million dollars, a sum that PAG General Manager Joe Mesa said was just recently guaranteed.

So, we have to ask: What is really going on? Who is pushing the privatization of PAG? Why are these facts still not enough to convince them of the obvious - that to privatize the only port of an import-based island economy is to open the door to danger, and open it widely?

Answers to these questions may lie behind the door of another public agency being targeted for privatization – the Guam Waterworks Authority (GWA). I have been following the privatization of both GWA and PAG close enough to figure out that what is going on is a PR campaign designed to distract us with complaints about mass inefficiencies at both agencies. But if we had access to cleaner information, we would know how some people tried desperately hard to privatize GWA under the concession model - the exact model of water privatization that has failed over and over again around the world. We would know how the Consolidated Commission on Utilities (CCU) consistently dismissed our concerns, pushing so hard for a poorly-thought-out bill that would have had us lose our natural resource to the hands of an outsider-controlled company profiting at our expense. We would know how the same small but influential group - the Chamber of Commerce – is behind the push to privatize both agencies even if privatization schemes will not improve either of their operations over the long haul. And because this group's interests so closely mirror the editorial position of the Pacific Daily News, we are not surprised that the real news – news of GWA improvements, of CCU's underhanded actions, and now of the potential devastating consequences of PAG privatization – is not getting out.

Despite the fact that the PDN appears hell bent on selling us the idea that privatization – apparently, of everything - is in our best interest, some of us have not been tricked. We know there is so much we are not being told. We know that those pushing to privatize PAG are not all that interested in the sustainable development of our island and are quite satisfied that Guam stays an only import-based economy. Guam is an undeveloped island economy that has been strangled by outside interests for far too long; we must be wary of those set on keeping it this way. People of Guam: it is high time we export something. Let's start with some indignation.

On the Myth of Military Money

People of Guam: the transfer of thousands of US marines and their dependents to our island should give our moral outrage a new lease of life. And although it will have devastating consequences on all levels – social, moral, cultural, political, ecological – it seems as if only money matters. So, let's start there.

Fact: of the 10.3B settled upon by the US and Japan, we have yet to find out exactly how much of this is going to be used to improve and upgrade local infrastructure, or in what ways. Will money go directly toward capital improvement projects or will they be spent unwisely on more privatization efforts like those we still see being pushed from the top-down at both the Guam Waterworks Authority and the Port Authority of Guam?

Fact: military communities are self-contained communities; their dollars stay mostly on base. Dollars that make it out will go where they always go - to the sex industry (porn shops, massage parlors, etc.) As case studies from various places indicate, one example being Hawai'i, US military build-up does not benefit common people. The big bucks go to big business, which are privileged over locally owned small businesses. Big, mainland-controlled companies make their money and leave. They receive corporate welfare: for example, they will be given qualifying certificates (QCs) allowing them twenty years of tax evasion in exchange for participating in Guam's economic development. Though these come with clauses requiring the training of locals to take over management of these businesses, this doesn't happen. These companies are not subject to local accountability and do not pay their share of taxes. The locals they hire will not earn a living wage. Instead, we'll get menial jobs at which we will earn too little to pay taxes and contribute to the general treasury.

Outside contractors brought here for construction projects resulting from the buildup will most likely work solely on base, remain unaccountable to us, and contribute nothing to our treasury. If we paid better attention, we would be making noise about the fact that U.S. Defense officials have already awarded two multi-million dollar contracts to two

US mainland-based companies for construction projects here in Guam. TEC, Inc. Joint Venture, a company based out of Charlottesville, Virginia, has received a $40 million military contract to do work here, Saipan and Hawai'i. Epsilon Systems Solutions, Inc., a company based out of San Diego, California was awarded $5.7 million dollars to repair and upgrade naval berthing barges here and elsewhere. Already we see how this game works. So, where are our local players? Could local companies have done some of this work? These contracts are supposedly competitive, so where was the Request for Proposal? I blinked and must have missed it.

In the end, we must ask: who benefits from this transfer, really? Perhaps the best way to find this answer is to look to the group pushing so hard for it – elite members of our business community, in particular, the local Chamber of Commerce. This group has been pushing the mass privatization of Guam as well. It is they, not the common people, who stand to benefit from this buildup. We must remember that the real engine of our economy is not the Chamber, but the relatively disempowered, locally-owned small business sector – the very sector that will be threatened by this transfer. What we are witnessing is a plan to keep the wealthy rich and the rest of us without. And we should not be surprised; people with almost only profit on the brain often have interests that endanger the true welfare of the wider community.

Our leaders are standing almost blindly behind this transfer, moving fast and against the wind of what small hope has survived in our hearts for some sort of decolonized future. It is more urgent than ever for those of us who know to act and for those of us who are just plain tired to shake the sleep off.

Too much is at stake. And the numbers just aren't adding up.

The Best Weapon in Our Arsenal

Two weeks ago, top US defense officials met with Guam statesmen and declared little more than that the US plans to make a permanent military outpost of Guam. Department of Defense Undersecretary Lawless met with local leaders and said, in effect, nothing. Despite the fact that this military realignment will change our island forever, we were told we must wait until the federal government hands down its master plan.

According to Undersecretary Lawless, and some of our own politicians (who are being far too polite about this whole exchange), we are expected to wait on a master plan to come down from US federal departments that will be beneficial to us. We are waiting, then, on a miracle. These are the same federal departments that purposefully killed a presidential directive handed down in 1975 by then President Ford demanding Guam be given a commonwealth status ‘no less favorable’ than the one negotiated between the US and the Northern Marianas.

As a signatory of the United Nations Charter, the US accepted as “a sacred trust” the obligation to see that the native inhabitants of Guam attain a full measure of self-government. Put simply, the international community charged the US with the responsibility to aid the Chamoru of Guam to exercise our legal right to self determination. More than forty years ago, UN Resolution 1514 was passed, declaring that ‘all peoples have the right to self-determination; by virtue of that right they freely determine their political status and freely pursue their economic, social and cultural development.’ It declared further that “immediate steps shall be taken, in Trust and Non-Self-Governing Territories or all other territories which have not yet attained independence, to transfer all powers to the peoples of those territories, without any conditions or reservations, in accordance with their freely expressed will and desire.”

But the US has not acted in good faith. It has stunted Guam’s chances to become a sovereign state by actively discouraging the self determination process. It has hindered our ability to develop a real economy by various oppressive and colonial policies. One such policy was the national security clearance policy, which created a black hole of lost economic opportunities for Guam and was not lifted until 1962. By denying us the right to control immigration laws for ourselves, the US has used immigration as a colonial tool to dilute the native population, presumably to push self determination for the Chamoru even further out of reach. Over the last fifty years, our protectorate has not done a very good job at protecting us.

And now, with this military realignment that will have us house still more US weapons of mass destruction with which to provoke China, our protectorate is literally putting us in harm's way, front and center.

A friend who read my editorial last week, on the myth of military money, said I sounded angry. Angry is not quite right. I am more outraged than angry and even more grieved than that. When are we going to see that the stakes are so devastatingly high now? And I do not mean just Guam. Our region is being over-militarized in the US' attempt to contain China. Our world is in a far more fragile state now because of the US-led War on Terror, which set out to accomplish peace through war. But we know. The building up of armies, munitions, and weapons of mass destruction cannot lead to peace. The seeds of aggression can never lead to the flowering of anything but violence. Yet this is the sales pitch from the powerful.

These days the integrity of our small but ancient civilization is endangered by the excesses of a country whose wartime budget is larger than that of the other nine leading military powers of the world, combined. Why are we not talking about this?

If we are quiet enough, we can hear it: the space between us filling up fast with all the things we are too afraid to say to each other.

Chamoru people: we are the bearers of a civilization more than 4,000 years old. Let's not forget that. Our memory may be the best weapon in our arsenal.

For Love of Our Children

Watching the Japanese army drag away ninety year olds nonviolently protesting the Koizumi administration's arrogant dismissal of their pleas for peace showed me what Chamoru survival might look like, even after the marines. Their demonstrations in last month's 61st anniversary of the Battle of Okinawa showed the world what nationhood looks like when it lives only in a people's minds. As far as they're concerned, they are the gatekeepers of the Ryukyu Kingdom, no matter that their borders have been bartered away by Japan since the end of the last world war. In their dissent they offer us everything. Theirs is a model of how not to become a cultural casualty just because a colonizer has come calling.

There may be nothing we can do to stop the US military realignment from flooding our island with 55,000 people from the outside. But by no means does this mean there is nothing we can do. We can extend both our hands and hold the line. Instead of buying the version of truth the Guam elite and media is selling, we can stop and think and remember. Start one serious project of introspection. See the writing on the wall for what it is – the signature of a colonial situation.

In the most recent uniform crime report (UCR) released in 2004 by the Guam police department, more than one hundred and sixty rapes were reported. More than one hundred fifty aggravated assaults. In our once matrilineal society, the rage of broken men is released through their fists on our women. In the same year, Chamoru families made up nearly 60% of the total incidences of family violence reported to the police. That's 472 out of 798 families. And the latter was a jump of more than two hundred cases of family violence from 2000. Quite a jump for a four year period. And these reflect only the adult population. Recorded juvenile offenses for the same year also point to Chamoru overrepresentation in violent crimes among youth, with our kids making up 176 of the total 291 offenses of 2004. That's roughly 60%. The UCR also indicated that Chamorus made up roughly 65% of all the drug abuse cases of 2004. That's 135 out of 207 cases. In the same year, the Bureau of Planning released the Guam Statistical Yearbook, showing Guam's unemployed population to be 4,710. Unsurprisingly, we also make up nearly half this population.

Figures like these make it no wonder that it is Chamorus who line almost every cell at both of Guam's correctional facilities - the Department of Corrections and the

Department of Youth Affairs. Figures like these bespeak an underlying reality of Chamoru dispossession. Based off the latest census data, which estimates the Chamoru population of Guam to be 37.1%, Chamoru representation in rates of violent crimes, family violence, drug abuse, and incarceration should not exceed this 37.1% mark. Because this is obviously not the case, any student of society would reasonably conclude that Chamorus today struggle to stand up under the weight of oppressive, colonial forces. And the weight has proven too much for many.

Down on the beach, another kind of incarceration on display.

Nearly every day at sunset, I run the three mile stretch of Tumon Bay known as Hotel Road. Around 6:30 p.m. the line of four-stars starts their dinner shows. Tahitian drums beat the air, Hawaiian hula floats across the stage. All along the beach, faces of Japanese tourists light up watching Chamoru teenagers perform Polynesian fire dances. Chamoru children chasing their tails in search of self. Cultural misappropriation on nightly display, making mockery of an indigenous identity challenged by a five-century colonization.

Meanwhile, our language sits on the edge of existence.

In April of last year a pioneer study of the Haya Cultural Heritage and Preservation Institute measured the extent to which our language is being used – or not used - in Chamoru homes in the south end of the island. Given that only one generation of Chamorus remain who both speak and understand the language fluently, the group reports that the language will die with this generation, unless serious measures are taken to stop it. According to cultural practitioner Anne Marie Arceo, who was intimately involved in the study, the last generation of fluent Chamorus is fifty year olds and above, born before or during World War II. Given that the life expectancy of Chamorus is roughly 78 years old, Arceo asserts that we are looking at a twenty-some year window to save the language from extinction.

This of course was a long time coming. Since the 19th century - from the Pacific Ocean to Indian Country - the US has used its schools to facilitate the extinction of native languages. American schools in Guam, both before 1941 and after 1945, were established to eradicate the Chamoru, tongue and person. To educate the old Chamoru out of the new American. The native out of the patriot. We have heard them too many times. The stories about our parents being scolded and punished for speaking Chamoru. The stories about our grandparents discontinuing its use with us because our success in life was tied to learning English only.

But the nastier lesson their schools taught was that their dreams were ours. That indigenous knowledge had no place in the new world. Collective Economics and Interdependence: make room for Excessive Individualism. The new chief. The accomplishment of more than sixty years of US education in Guam has been the dislocation of our Chamoru center - the fragmentation of our identity as an indigenous people who possess something distinct to offer humanity. As vehicles for our assimilation, American schools have attached to our longings alien aspirations for material wealth, money and power. How much of our creativity and our vision has already been laid to waste for the sake of these?

We may not be able to stop the relocation, but we can stop the dislocation. If we look carefully, we see the first pipes of our survival being fitted.

This spring in San Diego, California, members of the Sons and Daughters of Guam Club put on a conference they called Famoksaiyan: Decolonizing Chamoru Histories, Identities, and Futures. The first forum of its kind, Famoksaiyan pulled together mostly young Chamoru scholar-activists from across the continental US. Together, they broke down some pretty big pedagogical doors. Opened up a bigger space for decolonizing Chamoru theory, praxis, and politics. One tangible result from their gathering was a petition - signed by many international parties - addressed to Chairman Julian Hunte of the UN Special Committee on Decolonization and UN Secretary General Kofi Annan. The petition competently outlines how the current US military realignment of troops from Okinawa to Guam violates international law and endangers the right to self-determination vouchsafed to the Chamoru people under UN resolution 1514 of 1960.

Last week, another reason to hope reached my hearing.

As part of the closing ceremony of the Hurao Cultural summer camp last week, sixty five children chanted in fino' haya, the ancient language. The camp was a month-long language immersion program headed by a group of Chamoru teachers who volunteered their time to teach the kids everything from chant and weaving to oral history and the basic mechanics of the language. Though not yet an immersion school, it is the beginnings of one.

It is said that the ancient language – the precursor to modern Chamoru which blends the indigenous language with some Spanish - can only be understood by very old folks and ghosts. It warms me to think of them. Chamoru children. So beautifully disturbing the dead.

On a hill three minutes from my house, another pipe is being fitted for Chamoru survival.

On March 29, 2006, the Chamoru Land Trust signed over a lease for Oka Point - an eight acre piece of real estate in Tumon village - to the newly formed nonprofit organization Inadahen I Lina'la' I Kotturan Chamoru - Guardians of the Life of the Chamoru Culture. At a meeting with the Trust one month earlier, both the young and the elderly, both artists and attorneys, testified of the need for the land to build a Chamoru cultural center. The group has been up on the hill every weekend since April. Slowly clearing the property, stopping the bush cutters for the occasional story-telling session, chant, or meal. Breaking bread with both worlds.

As artists they are after a thing of incomparable beauty. A mirror in which - when this thing, this war, this clamor calms - a Chamoru face can still be found.

In truth, they remind me of Majnun. Of the Persian stories. Majnun - though he knew his beloved Leyli was pure spirit - was the lover desperate in the desert, trying to find her. Sift her from the sand.

On the hill, art looks more like armor. Like rocks to throw at a goddess of beauty we have tragically imported. For love of our children, they will kill her.

I will make it up there soon. I want to see for myself the taken-back beauty.

Knowing is (more than half) the Battle

In continued violation of international law, the US has yet to meaningfully engage local leaders on the true – and unspoken - ramifications of the transfer of thousands to Guam due to US military realignment in the Asia-Pacific region. In what has been described as a large-scale demonstration of military might, three US aircraft carriers – the USS Abraham Lincoln, the USS Kitty Hawk, and the USS Ronald Reagan – will convene off Guam waters this month for the military exercise Valiant Shield. The exercise and others like it to follow are important because, apparently, China and North Korea must be contained.

Carl Peterson of the local (but not so local) Chamber of Commerce had it right when he said, as reported by the Pacific Daily News last week, that "we don't know the specifics about what they're doing."

But we can guess.

Can the same government that has not yet cleaned up its widespread contamination of our island with pollutants including Agent Orange and Purple and nuclear fallout and waste from its horrific nuclear experiments in our region be up to much better now? Only last month, a US defense official informed us of how the US kept about 5,000 drums of Agent Purple here in an unknown location in 1952 in anticipation of use on the Korean peninsula. According to a researcher who participated in a military experiment in Cocos Island in 1966, the amount of dioxin at Andersen Air Force Base alone indicates, at least, US irresponsibility and, at worst, US crimes against humanity.

The findings of the research project on nuclear contamination commissioned by the 26th Guam Legislature, which detailed radioactive contamination in Guam between 1946 and 1958, should compel us to question current military exercises in our waters. Guam, 1200 miles west of the Marshall Islands, received nuclear fallout from more than ten of the sixty-six bombs dropped on Enewetak alone. In addition, US Military vessels flown above the plumes of Enewetak to measure radioactivity were flown to Guam and flushed out. Today, Apra Harbor and Cocos Island are only some of the places poisoned during these years. Just last year, the Guam Environmental Protection Agency warned us to be wary about fish we catch down south, particularly in the waters off Malesso Pier, which are contaminated with PCBs, dioxins that cause cancer and are potentially lethal in even small concentrations.

Is this the same military government we are expected now to rush to welcome? Are we really supposed to believe the lie that the danger is China? North Korea? If we would just pay attention, and set out on the study of everything we are not being told, we would figure out the obvious - that we, the people of Guam, have no natural enemies in the region. In fact, it is only now, in our now-active recruit of more US military presence here, that we are gaining enemies, enemies in the camp of those who understand that it is this feverish US military buildup - this insane idea that war will pave the way for peace - that is the real danger, clear and present.

Armament will lead only to more armament. To believe otherwise is to set out on a path that will only make final the defeat of humanity.

In the end, the loudest opinion in the room is that the US military is coming, period. If this is true, let's at least be smarter this time around. Let's hold our own leaders accountable and make them demand the US take immediate steps to clean up the already existing contaminations on our island leftover from World War II as well as fallout we received from the US bombing of the Marshall Islands, which has caused devastating loss of life among our people, who, even up to now, keep dying from related cancers.

Let's insist negotiations be done in a safe, international forum and a memorandum of understanding be drafted between the US government and GovGuam, holding the US responsible for future potential and actual damage to our ecosystem.

There is too much we do not know and too many of us keeping quiet.

The Pledge in the Region

Last week, as part of the games the US Department of Defense is playing in our region, an intercontinental ballistic missile (ICBM) ripped through the sky above Kwajalein in the Marshall Islands, hitting pre-determined targets on the atoll. According to the defense department, the purpose of the June 14 launching of Minuteman III was to continue assessing and demonstrating the effectiveness of its billion dollar weapon system. Since 2002, the US has been using the island to conduct similar IBM operations. In September of that year the US entered into a four-year, $626 million dollar contract with Bechtel and Lockheed Martin to support the operations, thereby continuing its half-century disregard for the integrity of the Marshallese archipelago.

After the last world war, the US began an intensive nuclear bombing campaign of the Marshall Islands, dropping 67 atomic and hydrogen bombs over the region. US scientists used the Marshallese people as guinea pigs, monitoring the effects of radiation in human bodies. These acts of aggression still haunt the Marshallese people, who continue to die from extraordinarily high rates of radioaction-related cancers, the most common being thyroid cancer. In one case, though they knew 72 hours before detonation that the wind direction had shifted toward inhabited islands, US defense officials chose not to warn the inhabitants. Earlier this year, at an international gathering of survivors of nuclear warfare, a Marshallese woman who was a child at the time when BRAVO was detonated described to the world how the deadly dust fell on the children playing with it.

I bring this is up in a shamelessly desperate attempt to wake us from the coffin of our inattention. To resist the enormity of the lie the Guam elite is telling: that the militarization of our island is not dangerous, that the US military is a well-meaning friend to our region.

This week I leave for Okinawa to meet with human rights workers from across the Asia-Pacific region for the 61st anniversary of the 1945 Battle of Okinawa, which robbed the world of more human life than any battle in history. I accepted the invitation on behalf of the Chamoru Nation, a group the Asian Peace Alliance of Japan recognizes as the people's resistance movement in Guam. From mainland Japan, Okinawa and the Philippines to Korea, Guam and Hawai'i – individuals and organizations will come together to further the global demilitarization movement. We will renew the pledge in the region: to encourage the withdrawal of exaggerated US military presence from all our homes, not some. As a group, we recognize that our solidarity is more urgent than ever in the face of how fast the militarization of our region is happening. We understand that the global war on terror is laying our world to waste and we are resolved to think up every way we can to save as much of it as possible.

Despite our best efforts, the US may well keep up its endless armament to fight its endless war. In its over-militarization of our region, the US may very well provoke the power(s) it means to contain. As the US piles it on, so too will China and North Korea (to the best of their ability). And we will all be in more danger than we were before.

But, if we concentrate, force ourselves and our loved ones into the light of a real scrutiny, we may survive. At the very least, we will know that we were not ourselves the ones throwing in the dirt in these fast-filling graves.

Field Notes from a Fact-Finding Mission: 1 of 3 or 5

I have just returned from a war zone. Though Okinawa makes up only 0.6% of all Japanese territory, it is home to 75% of the total US armed forces stationed in Japan. With US military bases occupying 20% of the island, the people of Okinawa are at every side reminded that they are prisoners of a war that has not ended. Despite the hype, the scheduled transfer of 8,000 marines from Okinawa to Guam will not relieve their burden. Instead, it marks only another bump in the road of the US-Japan relationship that has oppressed the people of Okinawa for more than half a century.

Because people in positions of power here favor only the stories told in numbers, let's start with some:

More than 4,790 criminal charges have been brought against US military personnel during the 34 years since Okinawa reverted to Japan in 1972. Among these are hundreds of rapes by US soldiers of Okinawan women. There are more, but for years, when Okinawa was under explicit US military occupation, Okinawans did not have any rights to sue or arrest suspects if they were US soldiers. After Okinawa was returned to Japan, Okinawans were subject to the judicial whims of both the US and Japan. Further, as Okinawan civil groups report, Japanese officials do not have the right to investigate within the area of US bases and therefore cannot arrest US soldiers for their crimes if they stay inside the base.

A compilation of documented postwar US military crimes against women in Okinawa, produced by the Okinawa Women Act against Military Violence group, lists in detail acts of US military aggression, violence, rape and gang rape since 1945 against the women of Okinawa. These are documented by year, date, description of crime committed, settlement (in any), and the number of information sources to confirm the incident. After raping and/or gang-raping these women, some soldiers (many of them marines), do different things with the bodies of the raped women they eventually murder. Some dump them in the rivers, some burn them alive in their cars. Women lucky (or unlucky) enough to survive these attacks, are haunted by a terror they cannot name.

Yet when women here gather to talk about how the influx of these same soldiers may affect our home, some men have nerve enough to get agitated with their gathering. One man displayed openly where he laid his allegiance - to the marines - whom he felt the women of Guam, in their concern for the wellbeing of our community, were unfairly disrespecting.

This is how the local elite block the truth. They control the conversation, fail to report information so immediately important, and paint - for the general population - local activists as a group of irrational, angry people without a point to make. Our point is this: we are being led to the slaughterhouse by politicians too afraid to be political, in the better sense of the word, to act with intention to protect civil society even and especially when it is difficult. I exclude media here because I have accepted the truth that dominant media in Guam is just a business in the business of making noise, not sense.

What do we really know about these marines? About the whole realignment? Not much. As Okinawan delegations come to Guam on fact-finding missions, what exactly are our leaders doing, besides waiting on a master plan to be handed down by the US defense department? Our senators, many of whom openly admitted that their meeting with Undersecretary of Defense Richard Lawless was empty of any real information, should take their cue from Okinawan statesmen and pay that occupied territory a visit. Go on a fact-finding mission of their own. Find out more about these alleged "family-oriented" marines that are coming.

This information, in and of itself, is insufficient to understand what is going on. The marines are a group of people whose training is meant to keep them combat-ready. At the edge of their sanity. Like attack dogs, they are trained at any instant to unleash aggression. This is why it is unreasonable to expect them to successfully integrate with a civilian population. This is why we should not be surprised at the level of societal violence they bring to civilian communities. Being kept this way - at every moment a single hair from brutality - and being expected to nonviolently integrate with a family-oriented society is an irreconcilable difference.

They are kept at ceaseless agitation on purpose. The government they proudly and faithfully serve counts on it.

The Pearl of Henoko

Two years ago this November, the power of the people went head to head with the governments of two of the most affluent countries in the world. On the afternoon of November 16, 2004, Okinawan activists aboard small boats and canoes set out to stop the 500-ton crane vessel commissioned by the central government to begin drilling of the sea bottom in the water off Henoko village for the construction of yet another US military base. Risking life and limb in what has become a tired scene. Tiny Okinawa takes on manic mainland Japan and master (the US).

Here's the skinny: the partner governments of Japan and the US plan to landfill the sea off Henoko, in eastern Okinawa, to build an airbase with a full runway estimated at 2500 meters long and 730 meters wide. According to Okinawan writer Yui Akiko, preliminary drilling demarcated 63 points at sea bottom inside and outside the coral reefs. Two years and a lot of sacrifice later, the people are still managing to hold back the Naha Defense Facilities Administration Bureau (NDFAB), the local arm charged to begin boring the sea floor.

In all of this, it is the elderly at the center of the struggle. Grandmothers and grandfathers dive in front of state-sponsored ships, driving them back. Seventy, eighty and ninety year olds shaming the state with a power beyond power lead the sit-ins and hunger strikes and human blockades in and out of the water. Their courage has moved the coastline. Down at the pier, fishermen from the north and south of Henoko have joined them. Their determination turned back the NDFAB thirty two times in a period of five months.

An unlikely allay has surfaced since then. The Okinawa dugong, a genetically isolated group of the saltwater manatee that feeds on seaweed in Henoko waters, has given them grounds to take their case to court. Using the US Endangered Species Act and the National Historic Preservation Act, civil groups for the protection of the dugong filed a lawsuit against Donald Rumsfeld in his official capacity as the Secretary of Defense and the US

Department of Defense, for reckless endangerment of the rare mammal. The jury is still out.

Having recently visited Henoko, I got a glimpse of this sea that moves these old folks. Its majesty, hidden and deep, has sustained the people of that village and surrounding ones for generations. Especially after the resources of the land were taken and turned into the military training grounds of Camp Schwab. This is why they are prepared to protect the sea at any cost. They are old enough to remember how, after the last world war, the US military seized large tracts of land from farmers and stripped them of their long agrarian society, making it virtually impossible to find work outside its bases.

Contrary to mainstream media messages, the plan to build this base is not new. According to the Okinawa Environmental Network, a former Ryukyu University professor discovered a document in the Okinawa Prefectural Archives revealing how the US has planned to build a base at Henoko since 1966. The document listed Henoko among those sites surveyed by the defense department at the height of the Vietnam War. According to this document, the US

Marine Corps had prepared the Henoko airbase's landfill design in January of that year.

The latest propaganda piece in the state arsenal is that the new offshore base at Henoko marks the fulfillment of a long-held hope of the people, who have for years called for the closure of another base in the center of Okinawa - Futenma. But the trick, in the end, was too cheap. These grandparents know better than to let their outrage over one base cloud their judgment of another.

As we in Guam brace ourselves for the buildup, let's learn from our friends in Okinawa who ably defend the more important border of their freedom. Their land, water and skies may be colonized but the stuff of their dreams is not. After decades of occupation, they still find Okinawan faces when they look in the mirror.

The pearl of Henoko is this:

Taking on Empire doesn't take extraordinary folk. Only extraordinary resolve.

Every Toast

In his June 28 address to the local Chamber of Commerce, Governor Camacho thanked the Chamber for its commitment to bringing the military back to Guam. In less than two weeks, he announced, the US will submit its master plan detailing the transfer of its Okinawa-ousted marines to Guam. The latest estimate is that by 2014, 35,000 military personnel and their dependents will set up shop in our thirty-some miles, inclusive of 17,000 marines and their dependents and 5,000 additional air force and navy personnel and their dependents. This plus an outside labor force estimated upwards of 20,000 people needed to fill workforce demands for construction projects the buildup will bring.

A habitual headline by now: Camacho and Chamber Break Bread.

As the Chamber is celebrated for its active recruitment of more military, let's not forget how this recruiting played out. For two years and counting, the Chamber has pushed a mass privatization agenda in our island. In close confidence with the Pacific Daily News (PDN), the Chamber has waged war in the form of relentless ruckus. Bombarding us with the story that everything must go. Half off. Hell, free. Sell every public asset. Telecommunications? Check. Power? Check. Water? We're working on it.

After all, who cares that the concession model of water privatization proposed for the Guam Waterworks Authority (GWA) has failed miserably in place after place - in the Philippines, in Bolivia, in South Africa, in Argentina, in Indonesia? Who cares that the Consolidated Commission on Utilities (CCU) led by Simon Sanchez paid private consultants $1.1 million to draft a bill so badly written that the people would not just lose – but lose big? Who even knows that the very model proposed for GWA was fashioned after the one that failed Manila? And not too long ago? There, after astronomical rate increases, one of the two private companies that won the bid for Manila's water systems, Maynilad, abandoned 6.5 million people when they backed out of a 25-year contract after just four years. But, at least in the first round, protest out-powered the Chamber.

Round two isn't looking too good. A recently approved private management contract (PMC) has taken over one of the two major divisions of GWA. Though we are asked to believe that the PMC is a good thing, we know better. We know all about its "hidden" fees. We know how Bill 220 works. How it is structured to allow the private manager to recover GRT, incurred and potential costs for operating and maintaining capital improvements - costs that will come out of our pockets. We know the nature of the PMC beast. How it diverts interest bearing dollars from required capital improvement projects to pay high-priced management consultants. Moreover, we know how the PMC creates redundancy at the management level, while failing to fill the critical positions of DRCs - the on site-managers GWA actually needs. And while we would never know it from the way PDN paints things, GWA has made bona fide improvements without privatization. In just three years, the agency has come under compliance with the Safe Drinking

Water Act and has brought the Ugum treatment plant and other troubled stations to 100% operation.

Of course, we are not expected to know any of this. What we are expected to do – rather, what the Chamber and the rest of the Guam elite is counting on – is that we go play with our toys. Leave the real world to the big boys. With big guns.

The boys and the guns are coming. Our governor just made it clear. But if he is going to toast the Chamber for its efforts, I would like to put my bid in early. For a bit bigger picture. What else is set for relocation to Guam from Okinawa?

Going by example, hundreds of rapes of our women. Noise from fighter jet planes so sharp it causes our women to give birth to premature babies. In 1997, a medical team discovered that the noise from military aircraft in Okinawa caused higher percentages of premature babies. It also found evidence of low frequency noise causing undetected but serious damage to local residents. According to Okinawan reports, about 1,000 residents around Kadena Air Base filed a lawsuit in 1982 against the Japanese government for exposure to noise pollution, demanding suspension of military flights over their residence. Though the court acknowledged that the noise was beyond acceptable levels, it could not pin accountability to any party because the Japanese government has no jurisdiction to suspend such flights, under US-Japan security treaties. Now there's an open skies policy. I almost forgot: every year a US military plane or helicopter may crash here. I'm told they do there.

But to go on like this might tempt us too close to cynicism. And that, we know, would lay our work to waste.

Time is already against us. Every toast of the Guam elite is a rude reminder.

A Word on the Raisins

Last week, a story wired by the Associated Press (AP) reminded us that it is unreasonable to expect the troops being transferred to Guam to nonviolently integrate into our community. Twenty miles south of Baghdad, US soldiers set another woman they raped on fire. This time along with three members of her family in an attempt to cover up the rape, in what is the sixth case under investigation involving alleged killings of Iraqi civilians by US troops.

Surprise, at this point, would only be embarrassing.

Though we know from Okinawan sources that rape and gang rape by US soldiers against civilian women there happen in the hundreds, our leaders are avoiding this like the plague. More than a week ago I dropped in every senator's box a compilation of hundreds of documented war crimes against women in Okinawa; I have yet to hear one word about it. The list of such crimes is long in other parts of our region as well. In South Korea, more than 30,000 crimes were committed by U.S. military personnel against Korean civilians in a short span of twenty years (1967-1987). According to Yu Jin Jeong, director of the Seoul-based National Campaign to Eradicate Crime by U.S. Troops in Korea, the crimes include the usual brutal rape and murder. Like her Okinawan counterpart Suzuyo Takazato (Director of the Okinawan Women Act Against Military Violence group), Yu Jin Jeong says that U.S. troops are protected by a Status of Forces Agreement (SOFA). SOFA, authoritative in both countries, provides US soldiers with immunity from prosecution for offenses committed while deployed in the country. The story is similar in the Philippines as well (with state-sanctioned death squads thrown in to the mix). But the story linking militarism and violence against women is an old one and needs nothing more from me.

I write this for us, who are being shielded from the truth that the rape of our women is not just possible, but inevitable. Marines are a group whose training de-sensitizes them. Dehumanizes them and us to them. Know this: we are the dark in their minds. The expendable backdrop in the game their government is playing with our lives and theirs.

The war being waged across our world - and our patience - is not only on obvious enemies – on Iraq, on Afghanistan, on the Pacific Theater, on women, on the poor. The men and women behind the war machine are also in its path. In this game, the foot soldiers are also the fodder.

We do not have to stretch to see this. How these troops are both predator and prey. How the war they are commissioned to fight has laid them to waste. Dried them up. Like classic raisins in the sun.

My rage has made room for them too.

On Oysters and Omissions

In typical form, the US Department of Defense recently awarded a multimillion dollar contract to a San Diego, California-based company, Epsilon Systems Solutions, Inc., for work that includes the repair and upgrade of naval berthing barges here in Guam.

To date, no environmental impact study has been done to determine how the barging – or any related activity tied to the massive military buildup - will affect Guam ecology. No federal study has been commissioned to investigate how the volatile increase of defense exercises on land or sea will strain the integrity of our natural environment. Worse still is this: environmental impact studies in the past have yet to dig deep enough. Have yet to expose the truthful extent to which the US military has contaminated both our land and water.

A report released by the Guam Environmental Protection Agency in September of 2000 revealed the findings of the

Guam Harbors Sediment Project, a joint study of the local Bureau of Planning and the National Oceanic and Atmospheric Administration. The report reveals, to a limited extent, how the US military contaminated various local harbors, the worst being Apra Harbor. Built to support naval operations after World War II, Apra Harbor included facilities for ship and nuclear submarine maintenance, repair, and supply, fuel transfer, nuclear and conventional weapon transfer, and other activities. The Guam Ship Repair Facility (SRF) in Inner Apra Harbor, developed and operated by the Navy after the war, produced possibly the most polluted sediments in any harbor in Guam, and, according to the report, maybe the world.

Sediments collected from Apra Harbor in Phase I of the project were identified as moderate to highly enriched with copper, lead, mercury, zinc, tin, polychlorinated biphenyls (PCBs), and polycyclic aromatic hydrocarbons (PAHs). 156 tissue samples from marine animals analyzed in Phase II of the project further revealed increases in arsenic, copper, lead, mercury, tin, and PCBs in Apra Harbor. Oysters from Apra, along with one octopus from there, showed levels of copper, zinc, and arsenic indicative of real health risk. But this is not where the report raises alarm. Copper, zinc, and arsenic, apparently, are not the metals the federal government favors. According to the report, the only enforceable standard for heavy metals in seafood is for organic mercury, which of course was not assessed in this study.

Another point of contention is this: though Inner Apra Harbor is recognized in the report as the worst contaminated of the sites surveyed, it was the only one not sampled for toxicity levels of PCBs, which we know are toxic in even small concentrations. As the report rightly states, PCBs are linked to cancer risks, disruption of women's reproductive function, neurobehavioral and developmental problems in children born to women exposed to PCBs, liver disease, diabetes, compromised immune function and thyroid effects.

Frighteningly familiar, no? Diabetes, lytico-bodig, cancer. All come calling on our people at horrifically high rates. But like the defense department, we ourselves are acting in typical form. Rolling over. Into these graves being readied for us from the outside, and in.

When the California company comes to berth the barges for the Navy, dredge the harbor, and expand the wharf, toxic sediments will re-suspend, release into the water column, and redistribute - temporarily but rapidly increasing the input of pollution into our food chain and the risk to human health, as acknowledged in the report.

The time to throw up our hands is upon us. Not in defeat, but in defiance. The graves are filling too fast.

Julian Aguon

Salt to the Soul Wound

In the most outrageous of recent developments, Nerissa Bretania-Schafer, Administrator of Research, Planning, and Evaluation with the Guam Public School System (GPSS), told a reporter from the military newspaper Stars and Stripes that GPSS plans to develop a new curriculum designed to educate Chamoru children about US military history, culture, and society. In hope of helping Chamorus deal with our potentially violent behavior. Citing the possibility of a rise in social violence with the relocation of 8,000 US marines and their dependents to Guam, Bretania-Schafer manages – with the flick of a wrist – to reverse the roles of aggressor and victim. Wrongly assign them. Turn history on its head.

According to her, the belief that the marines coming here wore out their welcome in Okinawa is wrong. She worries such stories might create among Chamorus an uncalled-for fear and confrontation. The curriculum, she says, will help offset stories of marines' violence and expose our children to all 'the good' they have done for Guam. A second suggestion is that the marines are less violent than Okinawan civilians because the marines are proportionately less likely than locals to be arrested.

Will someone please inform Stars and Stripes reporter Teri Weaver and our own Ms. Bretania-Schafer that the only reason this is so is because of the Status of Forces Agreement, which denies Okinawan and Japanese authorities the right to arrest US marines if they stay on base? That they are free to rape women in the hundreds, knowing they will get away with it as long as they can get back to their base before local police catch them?

Bretania-Schafer, speaking for GPSS, said the hope is to have pilot lesson plans ready by next school year.

I must have missed a step.

Is this the same GPSS that has headlined Guam news for the last two weeks? The GPSS so strapped for cash it has threatened to withhold teacher paychecks for the last two pay periods and counting?

At the time of this writing, GPSS is in need of $4.6 million dollars to keep the lights on, to keep the water running, and to cut checks to its teachers tomorrow, July 14, payday Friday.

The department currently owes more than $3 million dollars in payroll, close to $700,000 dollars to the Guam Retirement Fund, $860,000 dollars to the Guam Power Authority, and more than $120,000 dollars to the Guam Waterworks Authority.

Where does Bretania-Schafer intend to get the green? Certainly not from any local coffer. So will the money for the propaganda curriculum come from the US federal government? The way things stand now, doubtful. The US Department of Education is currently withholding $37.5 million dollars in grant money from GPSS over concerns of the local agency's alleged mismanaging of federal funds. To date, no solution has been found and more than seven hundred federally funded employees stand to lose their jobs.

But the numbers are nothing. In this story, the cake that counts is everything else. All the assumptions scattered across the article like corpses.

The implication is that the curriculum will curb conflicts that may arise with the influx of thousands of US statesiders to Guam. That it will encourage our children's wide-armed embrace of the troops and their dependents by reducing their apprehension and erasing their stereotypes. It's simple really. What the curriculum will do is undermine a long-documented, power-imbalanced relationship between the US and Guam - between the abuser and the abused. Charging that the side in need of sensitivity training is the victim, not the perpetrator. Sounds like an old lesson to me. Chamoru, bad. U.S., good.

Last Tuesday, in an email, Spokesman for the Department of Defense Education Activity's Pacific office Charles Steitz writes:

"We applaud any efforts to increase the knowledge of all students, especially when they can learn more about their own history, cultural diversity and the geographical significance of their home."

Can someone please inform Mr. Steitz that his history is not ours? That Chamorus lay claim to a civilization more than three thousand years older than our colonizer? That US occupation of Guam is for all intents and purposes a blip on our anthropological radar?

A curriculum designed to make our children identify with the armed forces of our colonizer is not one we are interested in.

But to be fair, Mr. Steitz is not all wrong. The last part of his email is spot on.

The curriculum - if we can we call it by its name – is education for indoctrination. Education for the last assimilation. It means only to continue a cycle of insidious trauma that has haunted us since the start of US occupation in 1898.*The geographical significance of their home.* Now this is something our children should learn well. So they are not later lured into the lie that they matter.

The first colonial lash came at the end of the Spanish-American War, which severed Guam from her natural archipelago. The 1898 Treaty of Paris broke the integrity of the Mariana Islands, splitting Chamorus of Guam from Chamorus of the northern Marianas. Under the treaty, the US got Guam and Germany got the territory now known as the Commonwealth of the Northern Mariana Islands.

After years of trying to eradicate the Chamoru language via a Speak English Only rule, the naval government hit the heart when, in 1919, an executive order forced Chamoru women to change their last names to that of their husbands upon marriage, along with their children's. The law also named the husband as head of household, thereby trampling our traditional family structure, which was markedly matrilineal. Its patriarchy has been one of the more potent of US poisons.

According to Dr. Patricia Taimanglo, these things have facilitated the dislocation of our indigenous center, causing us what is clinically called an intergenerational transmission of trauma. As people of an oral tradition of story-telling to relate our collective history, traditions, and genealogy, hearing the stories of our ancestor's horrific oppression has transmitted the pain of the stories to us as listeners. Taimanglo, whose dissertation is an exploratory study of community trauma among Chamorus, maintains that we suffer the burden of an unresolved, historical experience of humiliation, oppression, and subjugation. Part of the rage that rips us apart today, she asserts, is fury for our ancestors.

Is it any wonder, then, that we are overrepresented not only in the local prison, but also in the line at Mental Health and Social Services? According to local experts in the field, Chamorus continue to be overrepresented in psychosocial illness, including alcohol and substance abuse, violent crimes of homicide, suicide, and rape, juvenile delinquency and family violence. Chamoru innards strewn out all over the land. Today, of the 166 clients admitted to the Guam Adult Drug Court since August 2004, 70% are Chamoru.

We suffer what psychologists call the soul-wound, or the core suffering by indigenous peoples who have undergone violent and oppressive colonization for several centuries. This theory, advanced in the 90s in Indian Country by Duran and Duran, suggests that our internalization of or identification with our oppressors has had an adverse affect on our self-worth. Through forced assimilation, Dr. Taimanglo says, our self-image sinks to despair equal to self-hatred, which we both internalize and externalize. In her professional opinion, the mental health concerns affecting Chamorus in addition to the soul wound include the pains of loss and neglect, intergenerational post traumatic stress and the stress of maintaining our cultural identity amid volatile cultural transition. She has covered these themes quite capably and to elaborate on these here would not serve our immediate need. What we need now is the nerve to ask our questions.

Like this. Is it not enough that we already offer up our loved ones to our colonizer's wars in record numbers? Vietnam, Korea, the Gulf? In Vietnam alone, our killed in action (KIA) rate, per capita, was near three times the national average and twice that of the leading state, as reported by veterans in 1996 in *Vietnam Shadow.* Today our men and women are away from us again, this time for the war on terror. How many of us are in Iraq now, Korea, the Horn of Africa?

The new curriculum is not so new. It only adds salt to the soul-wound. Only breaks the knees of an already genuflecting people. If we allow the new lessons to infiltrate our already colonized curriculum let's, at the very least, not act surprised when our children come home from school but never come home.

Today's curriculum is colonialist enough. Enough an education for assimilation. Let's not be hoodwinked. The new one moves in only for the kill.

A much smarter investment of GPPS time and money would be to look into another kind of curriculum altogether. One that teaches our children about the consequences of excessive individualism and unrestrained capitalism and that shows them a better way to be in the world. It could help them retrieve what we have lost – healthy life practices of collective economics and community-based production. Make of them future participants in the rescue of humanity from unsustainable development. Bring us back to the land from which we have been separated since our reoccupation at the close of World War II.

In its recapture of Guam, the US leveled our paramount villages, dropping near five hundred tons of ordnance on Guam. The villages of Hagåtna, Sumay, Agat, Asan, and Piti were obliterated. Tumon, Tamuning and Yigo too. After the bombs, mass land-grabbing resulted in US control of more than sixty percent of the island. Whole families and villages were uprooted, forced off prime land used to produce food for the entire population. Driven from rice fields and coconut groves that produced copra. Removed from traditional fishing areas and relocated to small parcels of land inadequate for farming or fishing. The introduction of a competitive, American-modeled cash economy – aside from bringing in thousands of foreign construction workers to dwarf the Chamoru population – abruptly ended thousands of years of subsistence farming and trade. It is no wonder, then, that Guam today is an almost entirely import-based economy. Our estrangement from the land and sea – aside from creating a dependence on the US military for work – makes us susceptible to very painful exploitation. To very bad policy like privatization.

The clearest example I can think of is the potential privatization of the Port Authority of Guam, through which almost all goods come here. Once sold, the private company controlling our one and only commercial port – monopolizing our market – could put us all in very real danger. As it stands now, lacking an economy of our own, we would not survive more than a month from within. We'd starve. So a curriculum that teaches our children the ways of sustainable development – adding farming and fishing to their other lessons - could help undo a historical strategy of Chamoru dispossession. This is worth looking into.

Another program worth exploring is immersion schools. Schools at which our children learn in the native tongue.

Since they were first developed in Aotearoa (New Zealand) by Maori leaders in 1982, immersion language schools have transmitted to indigenous Pacific Island children not only their native language but their native worldview. Which we know is far more suitable for addressing the problems that plague humanity. Immersion schools have also transmitted native children a sense of self-worth that prepares in them an inner shield, one that will help them fight off the forces of death at work in our racist world. The forces being globalized by US export culture – a culture of excessive individualism and conspicuous consumption.

In the end, there is only one thing to do with the nonsense that is the new curriculum. Throw it out a window. Preferably a high one.

The Fourth Medium

I am starting to think that the only way to make sense of what is going on around us is to stand on my head. Because these days it's all upside down. Topsy-turvy and turned around. A tiny but terrifyingly strong portion of humanity has barged into the living room of the world and rearranged the furniture. Knocked over words and spilled their meaning out. In this upside-down universe, peace is war. Intercontinental ballistic missiles (ICBMs) are peace keepers, weapons of mass destruction (WMDs) are instruments of deterrence, not provocation. The free market is God and humanity is, well, a nuisance.

Valiant Shield, widely celebrated as the largest joint military operation in the last decade, was just wrapped up off our waters. The US defense department told media that the exercise was part of a national strategy to strengthen joint military operations. The war games, as they have been called, aimed to secure US dominance of all three mediums of warfare - land, air, and sea. But the more interesting medium to me is the fourth. The one that no one here seems to be talking about.

A long-range planning document first released in 1998 by the US Space Command marks outer space as the fourth medium of warfare. Up for grabs. In its Joint Vision documents, the US Space Command declares space the new battlefield essential for the protection of US national interests and investment. According to General Howard Estes III, the US is the self-declared steward for military space. Estes asserts that the US must be prepared to exploit advantages of the new medium.

In contempt of the 1967 UN Outer Space Treaty, the 1972 UN Anti Ballistic Missile Treaty and the 2000 UN resolution known as the Prevention of Outer Space Arms Race Treaty, the US has managed to further burden a world desperate for diplomacy. Just war theory, international law, the United Nations itself. All thrown out a high window. Regardless of the fact that 163 other nations voted in favor of the last resolution, asking - in fact begging - the US to keep outer space a safe space. US contempt for international law seems to seep from every pore of the Joint Vision document, which makes it clear that the US alone has the right to control access to space and deny others [every other nation] the same right. Put simply, the US wants the right to attack - from outer space - any country on the face of the earth that may or may not pose any threat to its national security.

The right to launch a WMD whenever, wherever, on whomever. Pretty straightforward stuff.

Here's where it gets good. China - that apparent enemy of the free world - is the lie we in Guam are being force-fed from every direction. China is the boogie man in the Chamoru bedroom. He's going to get us.

But let's look at him in the light.

Though for centuries it stood at the height of human civilization, China today is trying to withstand the assault on its ancient civilization by the corporate globalization project. With more than a billion people, China rivals neighbor India for the most populated country on the planet, with more than 150 million people living below international poverty lines. In the north, water cut off to small-scale farmers is being re-directed to factories in urban centers making sneakers for US markets. The enormous Three Gorges Dam being built across the Yangtze River has displaced too much of the Chinese peasantry, just as similar dams built in India have displaced more than thirty million people in the last fifty years. Meanwhile, almost a million Chinese are living with HIV/AIDS, a disease no impoverished nation can currently afford to treat.

Yet, despite her array of afflictions, China is also the reason the global disarmament debate is deadlocked. Since 1998 (the same year the US released its vulgar Joint Vision, star wars document) China has insisted on maintaining the use of space for peaceful means. It is Washington that is banging down the galactic door to set up space-based global strike capability.

Our bedroom is darker than ever but the boogieman is not the only thing we are missing. The truth even easier to see, the truth no other light need touch, is this: the militarization of space will prove the final defeat of humanity. Nothing else. If we are going to survive, some re-arranging is in order. Some word reclamation.

Peace, for instance, is not war. No matter how hard they hammer.

Tinta: a note in passing

Exactly sixty two years ago today, thirty Chamorus from the village of Malesso were marched by the Japanese Imperial Army into an area called Tinta. On July 15, 1944, twenty five men and five women were forced inside a cave that Japanese soldiers then lobbed a series of hand grenades into. Chamoru bodies still moving afterward were stabbed by bayonets. The next day thirty more Chamorus from the same village were massacred by Japanese soldiers in another area called Faha. At the time of this writing, a bill seeking to secure $180 million in reparations from the US for war crimes the US forgave Japan decades ago – has recently passed two committees of the house of representatives and now awaits a floor vote. The latest from our non-voting representative is that no one knows when that might be. Half a century later, we continue to wait.

I went to Tinta yesterday to offer prayer. To chant. My mother's side is originally from that village - the Barcinas family of Malesso. Joaquin C. Barcinas, one of the fourteen who survived the Tinta massacre, is my mother's uncle. His great-grandfather, Ignacio, is the brother of Benita, my mother's great great-grandmother.

I went to break bread with the other world. To remember to hold my rage so that it is useful, not destructive. I went to ask for the wisdom that I may see past the deceptively clear outline of the enemy. See that it is not the US that must be attacked but rather its insatiable, imperial appetite - its military industrial complex endangering the entire planet. Chanting, I am reminded of something important, something worth writing down: I do not hate America. I am disappointed in her. I do not resent the American people but rather the American export - its culture of excess, consumption, individualism (its culture of nothing). The globalization of this culture of nothing is the only thing I want to blow up. Because it chokes the potentiality of humankind to take our next evolutionary step – maturation. Growing up. Growing out of the angst of our spiritual adolescence, which keeps us from seeing that our disunity is our truer transgression.

US occupation of Guam - like US occupation around the world – is putting an entire people in peril. If it succeeds – if we do not resist, if we are remade in its image – then the world will be robbed of our gift, of what the indigenous Chamoru possess in distinction to add to the world treasury. Without us, any of us, the world is without.

My world is in the infirmary. In critical condition. I write to shield her from a premature death. Because she is beautiful, because she is worth saving, because she is not dead yet. And because, after all this, I love her.[1]

Julian Aguon
July 2006

---

1. This paragraph is probably inspired by the writing of Arundhati Roy.

GLOSSARY OF ACRONYMS

Acquired Immunodeficiency Syndrome	AIDS
Asian Peace Alliance of Japan	APA-J
Associated Press	AP
Central Intelligence Agency	CIA
Commonwealth of the Northern Mariana Islands	CNMI
Consolidated Commission on Utilities	CCU
Department of Corrections	DOC
Department of Defense	DoD
Department of Youth Affairs	DYA
Environmental Protection Agency	EPA
Guam Power Authority	GPA
Guam Telephone Authority	GTA
Guam Ship Repair Facility	SRF
Guam Waterworks Authority	GWA
Human Immunodeficiency Virus	HIV

Intercontinental Ballistic Missile	ICBM
International Container Terminal Services	ICTSI
Naha Defense Facilities Administration Bureau	NDFAB
Non-Self-Governing Territory	NSGT
Oplan Batay Laya	OBL
Pacific Association of Radiation Survivors	PARS
Pacific Daily News	PDN
Polychlorinated Biphenyls	PCBs
Polycyclic Aromatic Hydrocarbons	PAHs
Port Authority of Guam	PAG
Private Management Contract	PMC
Qualifying Certificate	QC
Status of Forces Agreement	SOFA
United States Environmental Protection Agency	USEPA
United Nations	UN
United States	US
Weapons of Mass Destruction	WMDs

blue ocean press

presents two new special book series:

1898 Consciousness Studies Series

'The Club of 1898' Consciousness Studies – The Club of 1898 are areas affected by the 1898 Treaty of Paris that granted possession of Spanish colonies to the United States: The Philippine Islands, Guahan (Guam), Puerto Rico, and Cuba.

The Spiritual Traveler Series

"The Spiritual Traveler Series provides the reader with a new type of travel writing experience. Instead of simply looking at the sights, sounds, and tastes of a locale, the Spiritual Traveler allows the reader to experience the consciousness of a nation".

"A Tourist takes in the local sights; a Traveler sees the reality of a landscape."

From the 1898 Consciousness Studies Series

Just Left of the Setting Sun by Julian Aguon

Category: Essays – Asia Pacific Studies, Political Science, Sociology, Women's Studies
Edition: First; Specifications: Softcover, 6 x 9, 88 pages; (2006)
Price: $13.95; ISBN: 978-4-902837-32-3

Just Left of the Setting Sun is a collection of non-fiction essays by a young Chamoru scholar-activist from the island of Guam. These essays reflect the present-day reality of the indigenous people of the island of Guam.

This book is framed in the context of an island that exists amidst the many conflicts and contradictions of being "freed from colonialism" by another colonial power in 1898 and "liberated from wartime aggression" by a country that put in under a Naval Administration until the 1960s and who worked to eliminate the culture of the local people through forced assimilation and nominal citizenship.

This book is written to articulate the reality of the Chamoru people of Guam as an indigenous Pacific Island culture, an American minority group, and an island people threatened by the encroachment of globalization into their lives. These essays will cause the reader to think critically on the subjects of globalization, sustainable development, sustainable governance, cultural reclamation, and self-determination on Guam, amongst the indigenous and colonized peoples in the world, question the value of democracy if it is involuntarily imposed on a people. This book is especially relevant for the present state of the world.

Just Left of the Setting Sun is included in an academic series that we publish, 'The 1898 Consciousness Studies Series'. This series is a varied collection of essays on consciousness today in areas affected by the Spanish-American War and consequent possession by the United States. These include The Philippines, Guam, Puerto Rico, and Cuba.

From the 1898 Consciousness Studies Series
and
The Spiritual Traveler Series

Cuba Is a State of Mind (The Spiritual Traveler Vol. I)
by p.w. long with Juaquin Santiago and Elijo Truth

Category: Travel - Sociology, Cultural Studies, Political Science, Current Affairs, Spirituality
Edition: First; Specifications: Softcover, 6 x 9, 80 pages; (2006)
Price: $12.95; ISBN: 978-4-902837-18-8

In writing on travel to Cuba, the Spiritual Traveler decides to give a voice to the Cuban Silent Majority.

The Silent Majority in Cuba are:
Voices unheard in books about Cuba. We read about those who leave, but not about those who stay;
Mostly black, mulatto, and rural white;
Descendants of slaves;
Masses of uneducated servants and peasant class before the Revolution.
Those whose freedom was denied after their participation in the struggle during the Cuban War for Independence (1898);
Loyal to Fidel;
Most protective of the Revolution and subsequent Post-Revolutionary way of life so imbibed in African culture;
Most affected by the US Blockade and least likely to receive remittances from relatives in the US;
Those who would lose the most with a return to the Pre-Revolutionary status quo.

This is the first book to give voice to the Cuban Silent Majority, to hear their stories and know their consciousness. It gives future travelers to Cuba another perspective of Cuba to consider.

Some Upcoming Titles From
blue ocean press

How to Rule the World:
Lessons in Conquest for the Modern Prince
ISBN: 978-4-902837-00-5

Following in the satirical tradition of Niccolo Machiavelli (*The Prince*) and Jonathon Swift (*Gulliver's Travels/A Modest Proposal*), *How to Rule the World* provides a commentary on today's "modern world" and the "forces" that govern it. This is done in the voice of "civilization's" greatest supporter, an advisor to Prince.

How to Rule the World is a modern adaptation of Machiavelli's *The Prince*. The author provides the reader, the Prince, with a methodology of non-invasive influence and control that will grant him sovereignty over his or her desired target nation-state and eventually over the world at large.

How To Rule the World shows the modern Prince how to utilize "modern ideals" such as free trade, democratic governance, human rights, freedom and individual rights, rule of law, and free press to exert control over other nations and convince them to collaborate in their own domination and exploitation through their quest to do whatever is required of them to be accepted as "developed", "modern" nations.

This book advises a Prince on what is necessary to create an empire based on the sustainable exploitation of targeted nations and what the cost of a mismanaged and irresponsible campaign can be to the targeted nations, his own nation, and the world-at-large.

Computing Reality

ISBN: 978-4-902837-40-4

The theory of systems and cybernetics is based on three interacting phases of thinking. The first phase is to establish the premise of thinking, which becomes the epistemology of the theory/theorem under construction, and hence the language and logic of computing thought. The second phase is a relational formalism in terms of laws and quantitative logical symbolism that translate the epistemology into a given problem domain. Phase two can also be thought of as a logical construction on how epistemology can be ontologically transmitted to explain a phenomenon under study by the logic and language of computing. Phase three is the analysis and/or empirical investigation of the second phase in certain specific problems and issues. Phase three also gives rise to inferences and future outlook on the shape of things that emanates from the first two phases when applied to specific issues and problems under consideration. This phase is also known as the ontic or evidential level of cognitive realism. Thus the interrelationships between these three phases define the constructed analytical methodology for the issues and problems under study. Computing reality means the use of these three phases in an interactive and integrated way to achieve the analytical and empirical ends.

The idea of reality in the above systems and cybernetic sense of studying interactively integrated phenomenon means exactly this. Reality is the continuous regeneration of circular causation relations between the above three phases. Therefore, when we study certain real world problems/objects, we must consider the pertinent phases of the above three types in respect to studying such a problem.

To Order

blue ocean press books

For Individual Orders:

You can purchase and order blue ocean press books from your local bookstore.

You can also find them at online retailers such as the following:

http://www.amazon.com

http://www.barnesandnoble.com

http://www.bn.com

For Institutional Buyers, Booksellers, and Libraries:

Books can be acquired from the following distributors and wholesalers:

Ingram/ ipage

Phone: (Toll free) 1-800-937-0152, 1-800-234-6737

Ingram Library Services Inc.

Phone: (Toll free) 1-800-937-5300

Ingram International

Phone: 1-615-793-5000

(Canadian Toll free): 800 289-0687

(In the UK) Gardners Books Ltd.

Tel: 44(0)1323 5211555, (01323) 521777

Additional Ordering Questions:

For any questions on ordering books, please contact us at:

mail@aoishima-research.com or mail@blueoceanpublishing.com